Bert-Mary Who?

By

Bert-Mary Brady

RealTime Publishing
Limerick, Ireland

Copyright © by Bert-Mary Brady

All rights reserved. No part of this book may be reproduced or transmitted in any form or by any means, electronic or mechanical, including photocopying, recording or by any information storage and retrieval system, without written permission from the author or publisher.

First Edition

Cover: The cover was designed by Elizabeth Cuthrell, Digital Design student at Haney Technical Center, Lynn Haven, Florida.

ISBN: 978-1-84961-131-2
Published by RealTime Publishing – Limerick, Ireland

Printed in the United States of America and Europe

Acknowledgements

To Debbie Hoover, the most recent and most important person in my life today, who has helped and encouraged me to take on this project. To Janet Nicolet, who made this book, first a possibility and then a reality.

Dedication

This book is dedicated to my mother who helped shape my life and to my husband who made it possible to live a fulfilled life. Also, to all those special people who have touched my life over the years, both young and old, and have given me such wonderful memories.

To the Reader …

If you dare open the door to my mind and bid enter …
Don't laugh at what you see or hear or feel …
I give no claim to talent or wisdom,
Only to feelings and thoughts,
Never meant to be read,
Only to be said …

Bert-Mary ... Who?

All my life people have asked me how I got my name. I have often been tempted to respond that it was tattooed on my forehead when I was born. I couldn't understand why it was so confusing, why no one seemed to be able to get a handle on it. There are girls named Sally Mae, Betty Sue, Nancy Kate. What's so difficult with Bert-Mary. Was it the hyphen? When I was growing up other kids asked what the hyphen was for. I told them it was to sit on when I got tired. I could understand kids being curious but I could not believe it was so difficult for adults to accept it.

I have been called a multitude of variations of my name. I have been called Beth Mary, Mary Beth, Beth May and most unbelievable, Beth Israel. I even get mail to Mr. Bert Mary and Mr. Mary Bert. I guess it is logical to call a man Mary but not a women, Bert.

When I was twelve years old I had to be in a hospital for ten months. The morning nurses would wake each of us by glancing at our chart and call out our name. Just for fun I would lay there, pretending to be asleep, while the nurse called out different variations of my name. I wouldn't *wake up* until she finally got it right. The other girls in the ward got a kick out of the game and tried not to giggle.

In reality I was named after my grandmother. Her maiden name was Bertha Mary Gregory. Unfortunately she died before I was born so I never knew her. My mother told me a great deal about her and I have always been told I am very much like her. My mother said that I have her independent and humorous nature. She didn't like the name Bertha and wanted to be called Bert. My mother took her nickname, Bert, hyphenated it with Mary and gave me her maiden name, Gregory, for my middle name.

I have always loved my name. It has been a bit frustrating at times but it is unique, special, creative and I think it is beautiful. I have a feeling my mother created it because she sensed I too would be a bit different, maybe even a little unique, with a creative touch.

I was single way into my thirties so, of course, people would ask me why I hadn't gotten married yet. If you have been single past the expected age you are familiar with that question. You have to come up with clever answers. I always responded with the statement that I was looking for the perfect last name to go with the name I was given.

When I was thirty-seven, I found the perfect name and fortunately it was attached to the perfect man for me. Now, isn't this just the greatest name? The best is worth waiting for!

Bert-Mary Brady

My 76 Years with Polio

In October 1935 when I was two years old, my mother was trying to get me ready for bed. She would stand me up and I kept sitting down. She thought I was playing until she realized that I actually was unable to stand on my own.

It was not summer, which was thought to be the Polio season. So, at first, the doctors did not know what the problem was. Finally, I was diagnosed with Polio and quarantined at home.

At that time specialist had differing theories on what was the best treatment. Sister Kenny, in Australia, was having good results with massage therapy. My mother, who had some medical training, decided that approach seemed the most logical. Therefore, when I was three years old, I was hospitalized for treatment for six months of therapy treatment.

I was sent to a hospital in Ithaca, New York. That was not too far from where I was born in Oswego, New York, and lived until I was in fourth grade. The only thing I actually remember about my six months in that hospital was that my crib was right by the door that led to the sun porch. I also recall a little boy whose crib was across from me and who kept throwing his toys at me. I don't know whether it was because he liked me or didn't like me, but it always stuck in my memory.

When I left the hospital I wore a brace including knee and pelvic supports. Eventually, I graduated to just a short leg brace. I guess I was pretty active and liked to try out everything. I remember when I was in Kindergarten I came home rather upset one day. My mother noticed that I did not have a good day so she asked me what had happened. I told her that my teacher would not let me go on the jungle gym. My mother spoke to the teacher and explained to her what the doctors had told her. They had said it was good for me to try out the things I wanted to do because it would be better for me to fall and break a bone than it would be for me to be afraid to try to do things. The teacher replied that she couldn't watch, as she was so afraid for me. My mother told her if it bothers you to watch, look the other way.

When I was twelve years old I was hospitalized again for nine months. This time I had an ankle fusion so that I would no longer need to wear a brace. I also had extensive physical therapy.

That nine months in New York State Reconstruction Home in Haverstraw, NY was an interesting experience for me. Because in the small town of Goshen, NY, where I lived at the time, I was the only person with what was considered a handicap, as far as I could tell.

In the hospital, all of a sudden, I was surrounded with people of all ages who were so much worse off than I was. Suddenly, I became a changed person at twelve years. In the children's ward I was always getting into trouble. We had water fights at night. Since at that time I was one of only two who could walk, we had to supply all the other girls with the water. We also had wheel chair races in the basement where we were not allowed to go without a "pink lady", but we did. I think our best adventure for three of us in wheel chairs was our big "escape." We rolled off the grounds, expecting to get caught any minute. We continued down the steep hill to a nearby little village that was used for rehab training. We passed the administrator's house where his wife was gardening and waved to us as we went on by. Evidently, she was not concerned that no one was with us. We got to the village after a couple of mishaps and got our ice cream sodas. That was our one and only purpose of the escape. After the struggle of wheeling ourselves uphill with our stash of potato chips and other treats, we finally made it back without once being noticed.

So, for that amount of time, I felt like just every other kid my age. It took me years to regain that self-confidence and independence again. After I left the hospital, without the brace, I had to learn to walk all over again. At thirteen, along with the typical pre-teen problems, I had to try to regain my self-confidence and independence once again, after I had slipped back into my shell. It took me several years to make it out.

I had another problem most of my life. My one and only sister, who is two years older than I am. She was terribly jealous of me, and I realized that at a very early age. She felt I got much more attention than she did. In fact, in high school she yelled out at me and said she wished she had had Polio. She did everything she could think of to get more attention. Most of the things she did were negative. It always came between us.

I have considered my experience with Polio as mostly positive since I improved as the years passed by. I went on to teach kindergarten through second grade for thirty-five years. In the summers I was a camp counselor.

I got married at thirty-seven years of age when I met my husband who was retired from the Air Force. What drew us together was the fact that he, too, was a Polio survivor. He had had Bulbar Polio when he was a teenager. He said that one evening while eating dinner, all of a sudden he couldn't swallow and mashed potatoes came out of his nose. He was rushed to the hospital and had to wait in the hallway for an iron lung. All he remembers is that he was so hungry because he didn't get to finish his dinner. Just then, a nurse with a serving cart went by and asked him if he wanted something to drink. He said, "Yes," and took a cup of prune juice. For some unknown reason, when the iron lung arrived they discovered he didn't need it. I jokingly told him, "That was really strong prune juice."

When he tried to enlist in the service at eighteen, he was turned down because of the Polio. Finally, the third time he just didn't mention the disease and was accepted. He served two years in the Army, then went for two years of college, followed by joining the Air force and retired after twenty years. He went into insurance and real estate and that's when we met.

We were married for thirty-six years when he died of a massive heart attack. Up until then, we were able to alternate our health problems so that at least one of us was up and able to care for the other one.

Thirteen years ago I was diagnosed with Brittle diabetes, followed by kidney stones, and that same year discovered that I had cancer of the esophagus. I went through radiation and chemo treatments and got a new hairdo all at the same time.

About ten years ago I started having back problems. This was due to my shortage of the right leg.

Six years ago I was diagnosed with Post-Polio Syndrome (PPS). I did not take it seriously since I was never given any advice or recommendations of what I should do. I have noticed in the past few years increased weakness in my right leg.

Recently, when I read a copy of the Post-Polio News for the first time, I began wondering if my problems might be connected with PPS. I was fortunate to connect with Carolyn, the editor. We chatted on the phone and it was nice to be able to talk with someone who "speaks the same language" so to speak. I now get the PPS News, which I also enjoy. We do not have a support group in this area. That's when I began wondering how many of my problems might be connected with PPS. I was also curious as to what I should be doing to improve my situation.

About two years ago, I developed neuropathy in my feet. The curious thing about that is that my husband was diagnosed with neuropathy and ended up having to wear braces about twenty-two years ago. At first, the doctors had thought it might be PPS, but ruled that out. I also know of someone who had Polio as a child and has recently been diagnosed with neuropathy. Of course, mine is supposed to be connected with the diabetes, but it seems curious to me. I would be interested in knowing how many people, who have PPS, also have developed neuropathy.

One thing I have learned over the years is that the more challenges one has, the stronger they become, if they choose to see it that way. When I was teaching, I used to tell my students, "If you just keep working at something you will be able to find the answers. Things may not work out the way you had planned, but they will work out. Just keep trying. You may be surprised at the different directions new experiences can take you. Take each experience as learning ones."

By: Bert-Mary C. Brady

Sketches by 12-year old Bert-Mary
while in the New York State Reconstruction Home,
Haverstraw, New York - 1946

Attention! — Stretcher Brigad

It's The latest in fashion!

Bin Gregory '46

How Long Will Your Child Be Handicapped?

If you have a few minutes, please sit down and listen to me. I wish I could reach all of you personally. Since that is impossible, would you just pretend that I am sitting there with you and listen to what I have to say? I think perhaps, because I was once a "Handicapped Child," I can somehow help you to understand and help your child.

Of course, the most important thing is how you feel about what has happened to your child. For you to do what I ask, you must be a strong person. You must consider your child normal. No, I don't mean that you pretend this handicap does not exist. Quite the contrary. For this reason, and I cannot stress this too strongly, children with handicaps must be treated in normal, natural ways. They need scolding as much as love, punishment as much as praise. Either extreme can damage. Anyone who would like to interrupt here and point out that this is true of all children is welcome to do so. I heartily agree and this is the point I am trying to make. A handicapped child is one of all children.

Now, if you can accept this statement, then it will be half the battle won for it will be easier to help your child to understand that he is normal. Normal in that everyone has some kind of affliction in his own eyes, be it freckles, a crooked nose, the wrong color skin, or ears that stick out too much. No matter how ridiculous this may sound to you whose child may not be able to walk, see or, hear, to them it is most noticeable and as devastating. They are as concerned about it as your child is about his handicap. People, and a child is a person, are so worried about their own peculiarities that they hardly notice those of others. After all, it is only natural that people be more concerned with themselves than with others until they learn otherwise.

Don't get up and walk away now! You must believe me, I have known people who have been more miserable and have tormented themselves to an unbelievable extent over a set of so-call protruding teeth. And others I have known who have had to substitute a wheelchair for legs.

A physical difference must be faced and brought to the open. Your child must be helped to treat his difference openly and helped not to try to hide or cover it. A homely person cannot hide his face. He must live with it. So it is with any physical difference. It must be talked about, learned about and completely understood before it can be accepted.

For example, a person whom I know quite well did some research a few years ago on the history of Polio. This happened to be her area of interest. Knowing that she was only one of the millions who had Polio gave her the comfort of knowing that she was not the only one in the workforce faced with the problems that go along with that disease. She learned, too, that there were those who had died. She did not, though she could remember the times when she had wished she had. There were those who were completely dependent upon others. She was not. This helped her to see her situation in better proportion. This is an important step in accepting oneself and one's handicap.

She also discovered that it didn't hurt to be a little conceited about her difference. She was glad that she had something that distinguished her from the rest of the "mob," and yet gave her an affiliation with a group of whom she was better off than most. Also, in reading about Polio, she knew she had the facts. She learned that Polio victims are of normal intelligence, usually over-achievers, and were first discovered in Egypt. These points were good to know, not only for her own satisfaction, but here was something she had experienced first-hand. Knowing the facts gave her the ability to talk about Polio freely and intelligently with people who, through mere interest, wanted to discuss it with her, but might have shied away from doing so for fear of embarrassing her. One final thing, she realized that she must have an answer for both children and adults who ask the inevitable question "what happened to you?" She made it a simple answer that would satisfy them and yet not embarrass them for asking.

Much of her experience may not apply to your child now, but it sometimes takes many years to accept a handicap. For some people it takes a lifetime. Others never reach that point at all. The sooner one can accept one's handicap they, too, will be able to use that word and any other similar word in the past tense because it will no longer seem to apply to them. After all, a handicap is just a challenge. Everyone has at least one, and those who have only one are quite fortunate. But, once conquered will prepare a person for most any adjustment to be faced in future life. If you, as a parent, have learned this before your child, then their years of learning may not need to be quite so long or difficult.

Let me return to my friend long enough to tell you that the reason I know this girl so well is because she and I are one in the same. While I am disclosing secrets, I will admit too, that it has taken practically all of my years to develop the philosophy which I am trying to give you the benefit now. Because I have lived through it step-by-step, I feel that I am perhaps a bit more of an authority on the subject than if I had only an experience of working with handicapped children. One advantage is that my thinking is not influenced by feelings of pity for you or your child – understanding – yes! but not pity. Neither you nor your child can afford the luxury of pity.

I hope I have helped you because I know that a handicapped child needs, more than anything else, people who understand and know how and when to help. My greatest gift in life is that I have had that person for a mother. This makes it possible for me to talk with you now instead of twenty or forty years from now.

By: Bert-Mary Brady

Four Minutes to Spare

I am well known as a hoarder of souvenirs as well as a saver of thoughts and it is because of this I find it necessary to "clean house" thoroughly now and then, the souvenirs I sort and burn, the thoughts I put on paper.

I was in the midst of the former project, busily cleaning out a box of old letters and greeting cards when I found an envelope overflowing with valentines. I pensively tossed them one-by-one into the fire after nursing over each, reminiscently. The act of burning valentines suddenly became an ironic reminder of a childhood episode which I decided to put on paper – thus leaving the immediate project for later.

It was on February 14, 1942, the most frigid night of the year in Middletown, New York. Our apartment was on the second floor of a rather exhausted old building. The main floor housed a group of stores and squeezed in somewhere amidst them was a tiny door. This door led to a hollow little foyer lined with a row of mail boxes and bells just at the foot of the stairs. I remember them especially because they had made an immediate impression upon me when we first moved in. Our family had never lived in an apartment building, so I was fascinated by the electric buzzer which opened the main door, the Murphy bed which hid away in a closet, and the sundeck on the roof that was used for hanging laundry. It was quite an exciting change from the average, small town house and life we were used to.

Around 8:00 p.m., in a pint-sized apartment on the third floor, two women and two giggly sisters had just finished a welcome-home dinner. It was an odd time for an eleven-year and nine-year-old to be having their evening meal; at least it seemed so to us. It was exciting. The whole evening had been fun. It had been entirely out of routine. A friend, who we called "Miss Judy", had just come home from the hospital. Mother had fixed her dinner and decided that the three of us would go upstairs to her apartment and surprise her with it. Going to Miss Judy's was always a bit of a novelty.

Miss Judy was bedded on the couch and Mother was wiping up the after-dinner dishes. My sister, Pat, and I took this time to make the most of our first opportunity to explore the apartment. We had excused ourselves to go to the bathroom. The rooms all had the mystery and enchantment of a place inhabited by an eccentric spinster. Little did we know what our exploring would lead to that evening.

After sneaking here and there, we peeked into the bathroom. As we slipped the door open, smoke slithered out. We quickly pulled the door shut and ran to our mother, whispering to her that the bathroom was filled with smoke. We were more amazed than concerned, for though it was a surprise, it didn't seem to us too terribly unbelievable that Miss Judy's bathroom would be different from anyone else's. Mother must have thought us up to one of our games, for she merely said that the smoke would go away and for us to run along and keep Miss Judy company while she finished the dishes. Instead, we went back for a second look. The smoke was still there. It must have been at this point that we assumed the roles of investigators and proceeded to open more doors. When we came to the hall door and peered out, there was nothing to see. It was all black! Choking with smoke we suddenly had the feeling that this was something more than just an oddity of Miss Judy's apartment. I tugged at Pat and said, "Let's go get mother." When I saw the look in Pat's eyes, I knew she, too, had a feeling that something was really wrong.

I imagine it must have been the expression on our faces which convinced mother that we were not playing when we ran back telling her what we had seen. No matter what she suspected, she merely said, calmly, that she'd take a look. Going with us to the hall door, she glanced out, turned and softly said, "I think it might be a good idea if we went outside. It looks as if there might be some problem with the furnace. They changed the heating system today." Mother never once showed any fear or anxiety; she made the statement as if she were telling us it was time to go to bed. The instructions that followed were delivered in the same quiet, calm, matter-of-fact way. "Pat, you take Bert and go down to our apartment. Get your snowsuits and boots on, and put Mike (our dog) on a leash. I'll meet you there." As she was saying this she was helping Miss Judy off the couch and getting her into her coat. "I want you to take Miss Judy with you. You'll have to help her down the stairs. I'll be down as soon as I wake up the others. It seemed like the others were oblivious to whatever was happening. Fortunately, she thought of them and went to alert them as we started down the stairs.

The smoke thickened as we went down carefully, step by step, bracing each side of Miss Judy. She was quite a large woman to support, but it was just as well, as otherwise I think we would have run. Fear was quickly taking hold. When we got to our apartment, we left Miss Judy propped against the wall while we went in. As we opened the door, billows of black smoke rushed out. It was horrible. Mike was barking and whining, but it was too dense to see him, or anything else. Luckily, our snowsuits and mother's coat were hung by the door, so we got them without having to enter. We put on jackets, but didn't have time for more. We were able to get to the kitchen where Mike was and just then mother came. She told us to help Miss Judy down the stairway to the street and she would bring Mike, right behind us.

I guess we made quite a sight when we appeared at the door; Pat, Miss Judy and me. We just stood there almost frozen. I remember the first thing I saw was a huge piano hanging over our heads. A couple with their baby came down behind us but mother hadn't come down yet. A fireman suddenly spotted us and ran over trying to pull us away from the building and asking, "Where did you come from?" I pointed to the stairway and said, "Up there!" I was thinking it was a rather stupid question since it was the only entrance to the apartment building. Then he asked, in astonishment, "Is there anyone else up there?" "Yes, my mother and our dog," I cried out. I had no more than uttered it when mother, pulled by a yelping Mike, descended. Mother sighting all the fire trucks, realized the seriousness of the situation. Then she turned and said she had to go back up the stairs to get important papers and documents. The fireman shook his head vigorously, "Sorry lady, I can't let you or nobody go up there. Everything is about ready to collapse. With this he started to herd us away from the building. As we slid along the ice, we heard a crumbling crash and looking over our shoulders, we gasped as the stairs we had just come down, collapsed.

There was no time then to get the full impact of the fact that four minutes later there would have been no stairs to come down and within minutes after that, there was no center at all left to the building. We were hustled across the street to a house where they had taken others from the fire. As we walked in, I noticed what a large living room it was, and how pretty it was with plants on both sides. People were everywhere. Some crying, while others were just sitting. We added to that collection a crying baby, a disheveled couple in their sleepwear, a barking dog, two confused children, one wobbly woman and a worried mother.

As I sat there, I began to wonder what would happen next. We didn't know anyone. We didn't have any place to go. We had no money except for the $5.00 in mother's purse, no insurance, and only the clothes we wore. I tried to quiet Mike down, but he was nervous, frightened and coughing. We later learned that the fire had started right under our apartment and Mike had had the worst of it. His lungs were full of smoke. He was suffering, so that later we had to have him put to sleep. That was maybe the worst thing out of the whole experience.

Soon the short peacefulness in the room turned to confusion and activity. I remember they were moving something out of the back and I wondered what it was and why it was being moved. Mother must have been curious, too, and inquired. I overheard someone say we were in a funeral parlor and they were moving a body out of the building. The direction of the wind, it was feared, might spread the fire across the street to where we were. Suddenly, I thought that if they were moving a dead body out, why were they letting us sit there?

It seemed like hours, but actually it hadn't been long. By now, I knew that our apartment was gone, along with everything we had. I thought about the Shirley Temple dolls we had gotten for Christmas. I sat there thinking and hanging on to Mike, looking at the woman right across from me, holding a Valentine box of candy and huddled in her fur coat. It was funny to see how odd were the things people had either grabbed at the last minute, or had just happened to have in their hands as they fled out of the building.

My thinking gave way to listening to a fireman who had just come into the room. He had spoken to Miss Judy. Then Miss Judy spoke to mother. Mother turned to us and told us that the fireman was a friend of Miss Judy's and had invited us to go to his house. A taxi was going to try to get in close enough to pick us up, but we would have to walk a bit to meet it. We walked blocks. I was amazed because there were still crowds of people. The streets were icy and it was beginning to become more frightening. I wondered why so many people were so anxious to stand there in the bitter cold and watch us, almost eagerly and excited, as if it were a carnival or something. But, the next few weeks taught me a lot about people.

It must have been late by then, as it was very dark after we left the lights of the fire area. When we pulled up in front of the house, a woman was waiting at the door for us. There was a fire in the fireplace and everything looked peaceful and safe. Miss Judy, Pat and I were given sleepwear and put to bed. Mother sat up most of the night with Mrs. Sherholtz, talking and waiting for Mr. Sherholtz to return and give a report on the seriousness of the damage of the fire.

In the morning, the fire chief arrived to take mother to the ruins. As they climbed up an improvised ladder, the first thing she saw in the rubble was a glittering gold object frozen in ice. After chopping away at it, mother loosened a gold-framed picture of her mother. It was the only thing to be found that first day. Mother went down to the apartment ruins daily to see what could be salvaged. Pat and I were even allowed down once. Miss Judy offered Pat twenty-five cents for anything we could find of hers. We only found one thing for her, a little blue willow bowl. There had to be a constant police guard, as people were stealing left and right. They went through the shell of the building, pulling and ripping objects out of the ice, destroying things that might have been saved after the ice had thawed. Most of these fire vultures were adults, not children. Some things had been saved, but only because they had been frozen solid in the ice and were out of direct view of the scavengers. Mother chopped out a cut-glass cake plate, which had been a wedding present and it came out without a chip, while every other bit of china was destroyed. Another find was a little six-year-old Zenith radio with the cord burned off. Once repaired, it lasted us another six years. These, plus a few pieces of wedding silver and Pat's baby doll were all we were able to rescue.

As the weeks went by, kid-fashion, we enjoyed not having to go to school. The really sad thing at this point was the loss of our dog. Aside from that, things began to look up.

Mother's faculty and the Board of Education gave us a sizeable check to help with expenses. Everyone was on the look-out for an apartment for us, a war-time scarcity. Through the help of Mrs. Sherholtz, a county nurse, the Red Cross was contacted and boxes of clothing, dishes and bedding poured in. So many things were donated that after mother sorted out what would fit us and what we would need, we packed up boxes and took them to others in need. The news coverage of the young teacher, alone with two little girls, the youngest of whom was a polio survivor with braces, brought a great response from everyone. They were most generous and sincerely sympathetic.

Once an apartment was located, the problem of furnishing it came up. Again, things arrived from all directions. Our church sent over a brand new couch. The parents of the children in mother's class sent beds, other pieces of furniture and a huge braided rug for the living room. A little elderly lady came one day with some beautifully hand-made quilts for mother and a doll for me. It was amazing to see the unselfish concern that was shown to us. We met people who later became life-long friends.

We were happy to be settled in the new apartment. Mother went back to teaching and our unplanned school vacation, regretfully, was over, too. The first night in our new apartment, before we went to sleep, Mother said, "This has really been a worthwhile experience. We have had an opportunity to appreciate just a little of what is happening to many war-torn families. We are fortunate to have a home and have learned first-hand how wonderful people can be to complete strangers. Be sure to always remember this and how well God has taken care of us. Thank Him in your prayers tonight." She kissed us goodnight and tucked us into our new beds. Under the beds were our "emergency suitcases", which became a standard piece of equipment from that time on, just in case the time should ever come again when we might have only FOUR MINUTES TO SPARE!

By: Bert-Mary Brady

Smoke

I once read this quote "Visions I no longer see and smoke is only smoke to me". It made me remember an experience I had when I was nine years old.

Smoke is such a simplistic word yet it can have many complex meanings. It's all based on your encounter with smoke.

It can be a stimulant for mixed emotions. For some there is nothing more artistically beautiful than swirling smoke over a distant horizon and yet, to others the vision of smoke can be terrifying.

If one has never had cause to fear it, smoke is surpassed by none for its graceful beauty. The fragrance of a smoking pine fire, the smell of burning leaves in autumn, the scent of an open campfire – nothing is more invigorating to a lover of nature.

To the homeward traveler the sight of circling smoke escaping from the chimney tops brings him closer to his own awaiting hearth. There the warmth of a crackling fire and the smoke wreaths from a slippered man's pipe waits.

For others the blackness of booming smoke stacks from steel mills, the funnels of docked ships, the cinder, ash, the dust of city bricks. These are the city -- an urban man's "Manhattan Tower". The sunrise over the dusky horizon thrills the dabbling painter. The rolling rhythm of the smoking city backed by a midnight sky sets before the artist, a picture waiting the creator.

Just once, give smoke an association with fear and no longer does it hold its beauty. Let the smoke uncover a flaming home, a crumbling building, awake to see the embers of a lifetime smoldering by your feet. When the writhing smoke drifts away you find nothing.

Suddenly, smoke becomes a horror – a nightmare to be remembered always. Once you have reason to fear smoke, the mere suggestion of its presence causes panic and confusion. The realization that a thing of beauty can conceal ugliness and destruction, that is when you see the fickle side of smoke.

By: Bert-Mary Brady

The Lesson

I was a teacher once
For many, many years.
I tied shoes and patted heads
And wiped away the tears.

All types of children I've seen
Black and white and those between.
Happy faces, anxious faces, sad ones too.
Lonely ones, angry ones, just to name a few.

I tried to teach them how to be
Independent of you and me.
To expect to fall and stumble,
To learn to be humble.
To be patient, gentle and kind
To leave hate and anger behind.

How to read, how to write,
How to spell and be polite.
How to divide and multiply
And to try not to lie.

How to think, how to plan,
How to cope and to stand
Tall and proud with confidence,
To try to hurdle every fence.
To Stretch out beyond their reach,
That's what I tried to teach.

In the process I discovered that,
From everyone you chance to meet
And take the time to know,
Teaching is a two-way street
You also learn as you go.

By: Bert-Mary Brady

Self-Portrait by Bert-Mary, the Teacher

What Might Have Been

When I graduated from high school, I had planned on being a designer. I did not want to be a teacher because my mother and other relatives had been teachers and it appeared to me as being a very thankless job. No matter how much one loved working with people, especially children, it was very rewarding but . . . It was the "buts" I didn't want to have to deal with.

One of my cousins was an Industrial Arts teacher and he suggested I might enjoy majoring in that area. He pointed out that if you knew how things were made, it would make you a better designer, plus you would have a degree that you could fall back on, if needed.

Since I liked making things and had some artistic talent it sounded like a very logical idea. Therefore, I chose one of the top colleges for Industrial Arts in our country, which happened to be in the city where I had been born.

The college was NYSU at Oswego, New York. I had been offered a scholarship from the Polio Foundation and so, even though it was a teaching university, I decided that's where I would go.

The only thing my cousin hadn't told me was that girls didn't go into the IA programs -- I discovered that immediately upon my arrival at college. There was only one girl in the senior class and I would be the only other girl in the program, which meant that I would also be the only girl in all of my required shops and classes.

I quickly discovered that many students and some instructors believed that the only reason a girl would take IA, was to find a husband. I had to prove them wrong, so I developed a silent code never to date or ask help from anyone in my classes. A code I lived by all four years.

I thoroughly enjoyed all of my shops: wood, metal, ceramics, textile and printing. I wasn't afraid of any of the machines I learned to use, but I did develop a deep respect for each and every one. I also developed a great poker face. You can't imagine the teasing I had to put up with at first, but when I was invited to join the IA honor fraternity, as one of the four girls in the world to qualify to be a member, most of that all stopped.

I learned something else when it was time for me to do my student teaching. I discovered that I loved teaching and so I decided to be a teacher after all. I looked forward to teaching IA (also called shop). One of my training centers was kindergarten through sixth grade and the other was senior high school where the shop was in the old bus garage.

Unfortunately, when I moved to Florida and applied for a job they would not hire me as either an IA teacher, because I was a girl, or as an art teacher because I wasn't educated in art in Florida. They, did though, offer me a job in an elementary school, starting immediately, on the condition that I would go back to college and pick up some more required classes in elementary education.

This is how I became an elementary school teacher, primarily teaching in kindergarten through second grade, and obtained my Master's Degree in that area.

I loved my thirty-five years of teaching except for the "buts" ...

By: Bert-Mary Brady

The Unexpected

Over the years I've had the opportunity to know and work with many people, young and old. Often, I've been in a position to give advice. One of my most frequent pieces of advice has been "don't worry about what you are afraid might happen because something will sneak up behind you and be a complete surprise." I knew this to be true because I have witnessed it all through my own life.

Let me give you an example. I went to my doctor for a routine check-up. When all was finished, I asked him to wait and take a look at a little bump by my collarbone, which I had noticed recently. I discovered if I turned my head in one direction it disappeared. When I turned my head in the other direction, there it was.

My doctor started feeling the tissue around my neck. After a bit, he said, "You know this could be cancer, don't you?" I replied that it had never occurred to me. Surprised, stunned and completely unprepared for such a response, I sat there in shock.

Immediately, my doctor had his office call to make an appointment for me to see a throat specialist. The next week I met with that doctor. He took some blood samples of what was now referred to as the "mass." Then he scheduled for an upper CT scan for the next day. He said,

"We must assume this is cancerous until we can prove otherwise." He also wanted me to have exploratory surgery the following week on the throat and neck area and have a biopsy done of the "mass" area. This was the 21st of December. The next day he called to inform us that I had cancer of the esophagus. Evidently, the cancer had spread and that's what caused the cyst on my neck. He also told me he had contacted an oncologist and I should call him on Monday and make an appointment.

The following day, a Saturday, the oncologist called me at home and asked me if my husband and I could meet him and his wife at his office. He explained the office was closed for the holiday and he was leaving town, but wanted to meet with me first. So, on the 26th of December, we met. We were there for two hours while he explained the type of cancer I had and what my options were. It came down to radical surgery, which he explained in detail, or a combination of chemotherapy and radiation treatments. He recommended the latter, which would give me a 50-50 chance of success. No treatment at all would give me about six months to a year of survival. I noticed there were tears in my husband's eyes and I reached over and got him some tissues. Since I was still in shock I was calm and cool as a cucumber, as the saying goes.

I started my first chemotherapy two days later. It was a very relaxed setting. There were about six other women in the group. We were all hooked up to intravenous units. There was a huge window that looked out over woods with squirrels coming and going and birds stopping by for an occasional snack. It was very serene as we sat there and exchanged stories. We were there about four hours per session, once a month. Spouses were even allowed to come in until we got settled in.

The next week I began my radiation treatments. Those I had to have every day, five days a week for three months. These were nothing more than like having x-rays, until the last two treatments, which were done internally. Those were what the doctor referred to as "insurance", to make certain they got all of the cancer. Those two treatments were done in the hospital, where I was sedated and tubes were put down my throat.

All in all, it wasn't as bad as I had expected. I had nausea the first evening of the radiation treatment, but none thereafter. I had some aches and pains after the chemo sessions rather like when you have the flu. All the joints ached, but it only lasted for four days. I was tired and took naps with our dog, who was my constant companion and also enjoyed the daily naps. Oddly enough, a year later, she died completely unexpectedly of stomach cancer.

The hair didn't seem to be falling out for the first few months, but then it slowly started to show up in the shower and sink. Soon more and more fell out and I decided that I needed to get a wig. It was getting very thin and began looking terrible. I ordered a wig and had my hair trimmed evenly all over, which ended up being about an inch long. Some of the women at chemo group had their heads shaved, but I couldn't do that. It just seemed too radical.

Others wore wigs and a couple wore turbans. We discussed the pros and cons of the different options. One day when the doctor happened to walk by, one of the women stopped him and said she wanted to ask him a question. He had evidently overheard our discussion and replied, "I am not going to tell you who my hairdresser is. What he does with my hair is just between him and me!" We all had a good laugh.

By the end of May, I was through with all the treatments and follow-up visits and I was feeling very good. I was told I was at a high risk for a second cancer, but it has been *fifteen* years and I haven't even thought about that. I had a couple of check-ups for about two years and the doctors said they were convinced that we caught it in time. I truly believe faith, prayers and a firm belief in God can get you through anything, even the unexpected.

By: Bert-Mary Brady

Certainty

Some things are certain.
Grass is green, snow is white,
The sun is warm, stars are bright.
Clowns are funny … aren't they?

Winds blow, babies cry,
Rain is wet and flowers die.
Bees like honey, don't they?
Some things are certain!

By: Bert-Mary Brady

By the Bay

Pines and palms entangle
With Moss dropping down.
Shadows play along the sand and
Mix with needles on the ground.
Pelicans pose along the dock
As seagulls swoop on by.
Blue and white together
Fill the never ending sky.
Hear the birds chirping
Somewhere in the trees,
Feel the gentle touch of
The warm tropical breeze.

By: Bert-Mary Brady

First Night

The lights are dim, your stage is set,
Props are ready, commercials yet!
Tighten your belt, straighten your tie.
Take a deep breath and now stand by!

Remember this as you go on,
Barrymore said (I'm quoting John),
"And when I stand before you all
I wish to hell the curtain'd fall."

But while you wait I'd like to say
What everyone says before a play,
"Break a leg, Good luck too,"
I'm sure glad I'm not you!

By: Bert-Mary Brady

Fall

The leaves of trees, the foliage,
From the center of town, to the river's edge
Are painted, each a different hue
Colors no pallet ever knew,
Gold, orange, red and rust
Painted bold and painted thus,
This is the season called "Fall"
This is the time waited for by all.

By: Bert-Mary Brady

Painting by Bert-Mary Brady

Spring

The day broke warm once again
Erasing the chill just here.
A breath of breeze
Unstilled the trees
And held their fragrance near.

The hum of mowers sang out,
Together as if by plan,
The sun beamed down
Upon the ground,
Laughing as shadows ran.

The sun soon peeked one last time,
Then eased down behind the hill.
The day has passed,
It's shadows cast,
And yet I linger still!

By: Bert-Mary Brady

Coming of Night

Dusk is falling like a bellowing cape,
As all around me the night turns colder.
A blanket of stars is spread out before me.
What a wonderful sight,
Is the coming of night.

By: Bert-Mary Brady

Ode to the Night

I love the silence of the night.
Everything begins to seem so right
The mixed confusion of the day,
Gently begins to melt away.
Raindrops spatter on the pane,
The soft voice of falling rain.
All those quiet, subtle sounds,
A robe of stillness wraps around.
A time for thoughts to settle in,
Ideas for a new day begin,
Unleashing secrets no one knows.
The night is dark, a candle glows!
And now to sleep, the night will keep.

By: Bert-Mary Brady

Til Dusk

The sky is a wispy sheet of blue,
The ground is all covered with dew
The sun beats down on the sugar white sand
A lonely sailboat nudges toward land.
Here I wait 'neath a billowy tree
For my love to come and be by me.
Together we'll sit by the inlet bay
And share our thoughts 'til the close of day.
Then off we'll stroll in the hush of night
Down by the water's edge in the soft moonlight.

By: Bert-Mary Brady

Painting by: Bert-Mary Brady

November 22, 1963

They shot our President today
Shot the man who led our way.
The man whose smile and open hand,
Brought pride and honor to our land.
The man who stood before us all,
An idol, strong and straight and tall.

Oh God, let us pray …
They shot our President today.
Pray for the man who now lies dead,
Pray for the country he galently led.
Pray for his family whose hearts were stilled,
The moment he was so brutally killed.
Pray for the man who made hearts bleed,
And carries forever the sin of his deed.
Pray for the heads bowed so low,
Shaken and unbelieving this hideous blow.

One bullet fire, it is said.
Felled him as it entered his head.
They shot our President today,
Leaving the world Tear-stained and gray!

By: Bert-Mary Brady

Forgotten

Have you ever felt completely deserted?
No one coming to visit anymore.
Isolated, empty, horribly alone.
Waiting, lost, yet no one calls?
Feeling as if you are truly forgotten?
Remember, you are never, never really alone.
Look inside. You will find peace.
Someone will reach out and come,
Midst all the shadows and gloom
Open your doors and make room
Have patience, reach out
Someone is there, someone still cares.

By: Bert-Mary Brady

Painting by: Bert-Mary Brady

Quality versus Quantity

Happiness cannot be measured in terms of hours, months or years; it is something that must be measured in depth or quality. For a little bit of true happiness can be so much more gratifying than an infinity of mere contentment or mediocre happiness.

In the first place it is very rarely that one finds a person who has experienced happiness for a great length of time. Our world is one of too much confusion and chaos, with its tragedies of war and sickness to allow this.

Secondly, if one is so fortunate to find and keep happiness, for an extensive length of time, it is too likely that this happiness will turn to boredom and be taken for granted. In this case it will lose its beauty, thus becoming stagnant.

It is the ugliness of wars and death, the cruelty of destruction that makes a little happiness so much more important and meaningful than it would be otherwise. If one has never known sorrow and has never experienced agony, can he appreciate great happiness? Isn't it the distance between the extremes that makes each more meaningful?

Take for a moment a situation in which you were given the opportunity to relive a part of your life. But you were given only the choice between a two-month span in which you were happier than any other time of your life or a year of your life during which you were not unhappy but just moderately happy. Which of the two periods would you choose? Would the length of time mean so much to you that you would give up the chance of reliving your happiest time in life? Or would you feel that it is not the length of time that is important, but what one gets out of it?

This is a hard question to answer, for it depends so very much on the individual and which means more to you – quality of happiness, or the quantity of happiness. In my eyes, it is quality of happiness not quantity that counts, as in everything else.

By: Bert-Mary Brady

Time is What Times Does

It was once said that everyone's day is made up of but twenty-four hours, no more, no less. The author of this statement was being literal in his observation and in doing so he is quite right. But figuratively speaking it is not true. Some people try to get more out of a day than others and for them the day is never long enough. For others a day is often too long, with never enough to fill it.

To put it another way, if one can fill every minute to the brim, the day will be short and eventful; yet if empty minutes tick by, slowly, an hour can seem like a day. A day is like a month and a month like a year. Here is a contrast between a short day and a long day, but true enough, each has but twenty-four hours. Therefore, time cannot be measured in terms of hours and days, but by people, the importance it holds for them and what accomplishments they can complete in a certain amount of time. It is through this interpretation that time acquires elasticity.

Time's elastic quality is not only determined by people, but also by circumstances. If a day is bright and lends itself to many eventful activities then it can bring the fulfillments of many days or weeks in a mere twenty-four hour period. Take, on the other hand, a few gloomy hours of nothing and you will discover how amazingly long they can be. Though long, unrewarding.

When we say that time, with its flexibility can change a winter's hour into a summer's day we are merely stating that it is possible to transplant a person from a winter's hour symbolizing a monotonous period of time which seems double its actual length into a short, carefree day willed with 'warmth' and 'sunshine' and symbolized by the summer's day.

To a well-rounded and complete person most days are summer days. This is true because in one's completeness the individual is never without something to do. Being of this nature one finds the days not in proportion to the amount of work one has placed before one's self. Yet, at the end of such a day, this person is rewarded not with a feeling of incompleteness, but rather one of great accomplishments.

By: Bert-Mary Brady

Boredom is Just Another Sign of Frustration

Boredom has become quite a popular word in the vocabulary of Americans in the past few years. It signifies a growing trait in the people. This might be an outgrowth of the war years, or perhaps it is due to the end product of our Machine Age – leisure time. For a person with too much time on one's hand is susceptible to boredom.

But, whatever it may stem from, it is only too obvious that it is a dangerous trait. This restlessness, this desire for unobtainable escape from seemingly dull circumstances and these spasms of uninterestedness, show how people of today have become dependent upon factors outside of themselves for amusement and for obtaining happiness.

Boredom is just another sign of frustration. It indicates a lacking of creativeness and ingenuity within an individual. One should always be able to find interest in something, if only to enjoy doing nothing – as long as one is not bored. For nothing can ever be dull if one has enough within one's self to project into any and all circumstances. When one is lacking something one is apt to become frustrated because this person is searching in vain and is constantly being defeated.

A well-rounded person, with the ability to make interesting every meeting, association and circumstance realizes that there is no one of so little importance that one can be ignored or made an enemy of. Thus, one finds in each person some characteristics that one can enjoy. This person also has learned that the most important things in life are the simple and natural things.

An individual who can find interest in such things as a setting sun, listening to the pattering of rain on a tin roof, or watching people pass on a street corner would never find one's self completely at loss of *what to do*! In respect, this person will not know frustration, in this phase, anyway.

By: Bert-Mary Brady

The City

Does the city ever really sleep?
If so, why do lights silently peek
Through scattered windows here and there
While streets are dark and bare,
Tall buildings every where
Stretching high into the shadowed sky.
Traffic whizzing back and forth,
Some heading south and others north.
But, if the city does sleep again,
Do you ever wonder when?

By: Bert-Mary Brady

Painting by: Bert-Mary Brady

Sitting on Dynamite

When my sister, Pat, married her husband, Rocky, and his four year old son, George, she was only twenty years old and it was quite an undertaking. They lived with his parents which, made things a bit less than desirable, but it worked out. Finally after three years they found an apartment with lots of room and many young couples around them. Most exciting of all was they had their first baby. When Pat called mom to tell her she was pregnant, mom told her she knew and that it was going to be a blonde girl. Sure enough, months later, a blonde baby girl, who they called Ruth-Ann, was born. It was fun moving into a brand new place. Now, George went to a new school, and she was home all day enjoying their baby and getting to know their new neighbors. They had been so isolated before.

It was just before Christmas that winter when they had their first real taste of anguish. Her husband came home from work one day and found Pat doubled up in agony. He rushed her to the hospital with what turned out to be a ruptured appendix. Peritonitis had set in. For four days she balanced between life and death while Rocky was taking care of the new baby and George, who was now eight years old, while trying to prepare my mother and me, now living in Florida, for the possibility of having to fly north.

Soon, thankfully, Pat recuperated. Not only were things back to normal but they learned that Pat was pregnant again. This was bright news after all they had been through. They were expecting a boy. Mom did not predict this one. Then, after nine months came their first real tragedy. Their baby was a still born boy. Pat had a healthy pregnancy but a complicated delivery where peritonitis again set in, which meant many blood transfusions and intravenous feedings. Pat was in the hospital for quite some time 0and dreaded having to go home and put all the baby things away. But, she didn't put them too far away because she was determined to have another baby boy.

She got her wish on Halloween night the following year, almost! She gave birth to another baby girl. Not the boy they had hoped for but a beautiful baby, blonde girl which mom also predicted exactly. They named her Tania-Marie.

A little over a year later Pat was getting Ruth-Ann ready for Kindergarten and George, who was now going into third grade, ready for school, Pat got a slight suspicion that she might be pregnant again. She told Rocky and they dropped the kids off at school and went to see Dr. Sam and he confirmed the pregnancy. He asked Pat why she hadn't just called her mother to confirm it, since she had been right two out of three times. Pat and Rocky laughed and explained they had to come to him because Rocky had a mole on his back that was bothering him and wanted him to look at it. Dr. Sam checked out the mole and referred him to a surgeon to have it removed. It was removed and sent off for a biopsy.

The results came back a week later. It was malignant cancer, Melanoma. The doctors explained the treatments and surgeries that might be necessary. Rocky seemed to take it all quite calmly. We knew it was fatal. I remember when I was visiting Pat she asked me if I thought she should tell him. We decided to go along with the doctors and do whatever they thought best. It was one of the hardest things anyone had to live with. Knowing what is going to happen and not knowing how much Rocky suspected. Unfortunately we didn't have much time to talk about it. Immediately his condition progressed rapidly.

I had to fly back to Florida. My mother and I ran a private kindergarten and one of us had to be there at all times. If I went back it would free mom to fly north and be with Pat through all of this.

There were many trips to the cancer clinic. A few weeks later Rocky was hospitalized for the removal of a large malignant area around where the mole with hopes of arresting the spread of the cancer. The size of the skin area removed was comparable with that of a football. This was soon followed by another operation to determine more about to what degree the cancer had penetrated. When the cancer started creeping into the upper left leg, amputation was considered. Later that idea was rejected. The full extent of the condition was now evident. There was nothing more that could be done. From here on in, it was just a matter of time, drugs and endurance.

Pat started having false labor pains about her fifth month. Now there was the possibility of losing the baby. Pat said she felt like she was losing her sanity, too. Since Rocky could no longer work the financial situation was getting desperate.

Finally the dreaded night came when Rocky had to be rushed to the hospital. The doctors had warned us that when this happened it would be the beginning of the end. Pat called us. She said she hesitated to call because she was afraid that when Rocky saw mom he would know it was the end, but mom was on the next flight out. It was now a week before Christmas.

When mom arrived she collected the children from various neighbors, did all the housework and drove Pat back and forth to the hospital. Rocky had insisted in every conscious moment that Pat be right beside him. In the meantime, mom got things ready for Christmas for the children. She tried to bring some normalcy and a feeling of security to their home. Something they hadn't had for months.

The doctors kept saying it wouldn't be much longer. Often a call would come just after she got home telling Pat that she should return immediately as the time had come. She would get there and Rocky had revived. She said she suspected that he was trying to hang on until the baby was born.

Two days before Christmas, Rocky told the doctors he wanted to go home for Christmas. His doctor said he didn't have the heart to say no, but he warned that just a touch would be agony for him. Mom said they wondered how he could stand just being moved. How would the children react to it? What if he died at home? Mother said she and Pat just stared at each other in shock! But, of course, they agreed. When mom called me to give me an update she said it was like sitting on dynamite, not knowing which would happen first, Rocky's death or the baby's arrival. Mom had predicted a blonde baby boy.

He was brought home Christmas Eve. In the morning, in a wheel chair, we took Rocky into the living room to watch the children open their gifts. They were so ecstatic to have their dad home. Things went smoothly until Tania, the youngest, ran over to give him a hug. Immediately Rocky screamed out in excruciating pain. Tania was so frightened and cried pitifully. Finally they were able to calm her down and assured her that it was the pain that caused her dad to scream, not her. Later that afternoon, Rocky decided he had better go back to the hospital. He had been trying to stay for the birthday cake. It was Pat's 29th birthday. The tradition was to have her cake Christmas night.

For the next nine days Pat sat by Rocky's bed. The following day when mom went to pick Pat up, they were walking out the door when a nurse came running, telling them to go back. Rocky was dying. He died just a few minutes after they got to his side.

On the 20th day after Rocky died about 10:00 p.m., Pat called her doctor to tell him to meet her at the hospital. Walter was born at 11:00 p.m. on January 23rd, 1960 right on his original due date. He was fat, healthy and beautiful. He did not seem the least bit flustered by all the happenings that had preceded his birth.

The following week mom and the three children flew to Florida. Soon after, Pat, carrying their first baby boy in her arms, boarded the plane for Florida to join the rest of us to start a new life without Rocky. It is true, when God takes something, He does give you something in return.

By: Bert-Mary Brady

Young Love

On a rainy day, that's when it started.
When the sun shone bright, that's when they parted.
It was upside down from the very start.
But you can't tell that to the young of heart.

They laugh, they love, they dance and sing,
And they pledge themselves with a high school ring.
They quarrel and fight but it's over soon,
For logic is lost 'neath the magic moon.

They go side-by-side, as others do
Sharing all with each, both old and new.
And bright Spring bursts forth with a sun-filled day,
Then one of two walks away.

On a rainy day, that's when it started.
When the sun shone bright, that's when they parted.

By: Bert-Mary Brady

The Doubtful

How do I know, I can't help ask.
How do I know that this will last?
He seems so right for me, and yet
Tomorrow might make me forget.

Another's arms or artful charms,
A certain smile, after a while
Could give my heart a sudden start
And there I'd be, my heart so torn
Wishing that he were never born.

So what then? Do I go on
To other men forgetting what has been
How do I know I can't help ask?
How do I know this love last?

By: Bert-Mary Brady

Don't Believe It

Why doesn't he call?
He promised he would.
I listen and wait
As he said I should.

Why doesn't he call?
He did say he would
He's ever so apt
I'm certain he could.

Why doesn't he call?
I was sure he would.
And what if he does?
I'll hang up! ... I should!

By: Bert-Mary Brady

Let Me Be

I ask nothing of you,
Nothing to say, nothing to do!
Only this I ask, let me be.
Let me be, that's all I ask of thee.

But you will not listen,
You are always there to christen
Me, in to a new being.
Never, never seeing me!

I shout in whispers and you hear not.
I plead and you cry "rot!"
Have you not compassion?
Why do you have to try to fashion me?

Can't you just let me be me?

By: Bert-Mary Brady

The Idol

An idol silhouetted in his mind
Stood between them all the time,
Except, perhaps at first
When the idol, he thought he had found,
Broke and tumbled to the ground.

He was shattered, hurt and numb,
Holding his wounded heart open in his hand
Looking for someone to understand.
She was coming out of darkness,
Basking in the sun,
Tasting every minute with love for everyone.

They met, one lonely man, a girl to understand.
He with his quiet, tender way, needing someone so much.
She, knowing, feeling, answering with gentle touch,
And love, did they find love?

Time and distance came between
Thoughts and people intervened.
Many ugly words were said.
The idol took its place once more
And quickly closed the door.

Now she was shattered, hurt and numb,
Holding her wounded heart in her hand,
Looking for someone to understand.
They met again.

She warmed to his quick smile, the old familiar touch.
She had needed him so long, so much.
But he claimed he never knew her.
She had changed somehow, he said
Speaking of what she should be, instead.

How, she wondered can anyone shine
In the shadow of an idol whose eyes always sparkle
In the sunlight of the mind?
While hers are dimmed by the strain of daily grind,
An idol who is always perfect in all her deeds,
While she is filled with human faults and needs?

Will they meet again, this time in the sun?
One lonely girl, a man to understand.
She in her babbling, confused way
Needing someone so much?
He knowing, feeling, answering with gentle touch?
And love, will they find love?

Or, will time and distance come between,
Thoughts and people intervene
And ugly words be said?
Or will they merely pass each by,
Letting the past outweigh
All that could be found today?

Is there no way to cross the gulf
To reach out and understand
And find something together hand-in-hand?
Couldn't they open their hearts
Forget the old dreams, the past,
Or, has the dye been cast?

By Bert-Mary Brady

The Parting

He brushed the curl from my cheek
And said "that bothered me."
I glanced up and flicked a smile
One, just for him to see.

He eased on across the room
Turning his back my way.
I rejoined my friends again
Thinking of what I'd say.

I listened to their chatter
Watching without a glance.
There was nothing to do but wait
Until he found the chance.

At last the chair beside me
Loomed naked in the crowd,
I held my breath and listened,
The silence seemed so loud.

I reached for a cigarette,
A hand held out a light,
As he looked into my eyes,
I knew that things were right.

In time we shared our secrets
And spoke of times gone by.
Whispered of the tears that fell
From others' careless lies.

May slipped in August
My heart sang out its song.
Then my eyes met his one day,
I knew things were wrong.

He brushed the tear from my cheek
And said, "It couldn't last"
I glanced up and forced a smile,
The time for tears had passed.

                                        By: Bert-Mary Brady

The Meeting

I wait for each moment
When he will be near.
Yet my work goes right on
As if he were here.

I think of him oh, a
Few thousand odd times,
As I watch the sun sink down
And night shadows climb.

Ever since that first night
When I glanced down the stairs
And caught his look midst
Those casual stares.

As I stood there a bit
Still not knowing his name
Or what he'd be like
And from where he came.

And odd feeling took hold
One I couldn't shake off.
My heart started to beat
Like a fluttering moth.

I knew I would love him,
If I didn't right then.
I knew he would speak
Though I didn't know when.

He spoke and I listened,
Oh, he didn't say much,
Just nonsense chatter
About nothing and such.

But I felt something else
It came from nowhere.
It was just loud enough
For him and I to share.

It is nothing you can explain
Or put your finger on,
But it's that little thing
Futures are built on!

By Bert-Mary Brady

Last Minute Thoughts

How do I know he is the right one? I've wandered so and liked so many?
What happens if tomorrow I glance around and find someone with whom I'd rather spend my time?
He has a lot of what I seek: warmth, kindness, sincerity.
With him I can be lost in conversation for hours and return feeling
Refreshed, a new person, a part of him.
When we are with others he makes me feel like a queen, his queen.
With a smile or a hand shake he warms the coldest heart and brings a smile to the somberist faces.
But still, there are others with qualities that he lacks.
He is far from dashing and not really too daring.
He is not a charmer or a great love by others' standards, I guess.
Yet, to me he is all of these.

Perhaps there is one, just one who has all talents combined,
But then, is that what I really want? The perfect mate?
How perfect am I? For everything he brings to me,
Should I not be able to match?
How selfish I am, asking for someone to give me so much
And never stop and think what I have to give?
Wouldn't it be more fulfilling if he needed me a bit?
If not needed, I could not exist. There is nothing greater for a woman than to feel needed.

So my dear, may you never know my doubts.
I will love you as you are and I will love you more for your shortcomings.
When you are afraid I will stand beside you and give you my strength.
If you should cry, I will kiss away your tears.
When you are lost and filled with doubts, I will take my hand
And press it on your heart, showing you, that to me, you are perfect in every way.
You may not be as intelligent as some or as passionate as others
But now, that I have thought a bit more, I would rather you be
Someone whom I can love with all the love I have been saving,
One who will love only me, for that is who you will be to me.

I want only to spend the rest of my life with you, making you happy,
Sharing your aches and pains, your happiness and disappointments,
Your dreams and joys. I will always be there for you and you alone.

By: Bert-Mary Brady

The Smile

He said "goodnight" one night
And started on his way, away
Then stopped and waved -- his wave.
She returned a smile – her smile.

He said "goodnight" next night
And started on his way, away.
Then stopped and waved – his wave,
She returned a smile – her smile.

He said "goodnight" third night
And started on his way, away.
Then he stopped and turned, returned
And she began to smile – that smile!

By: Bert-Mary Brady

A Man

He who wears a robe of egotistical complacency
Covering a self-centered devotion
Fed by continuous feelings of superiority
Which spring from alleged conceptions of indispensability
Is not a Man but merely thinks he is!

By the token above
There are few Men in the world today
But many who play the role and say
"I am a Man" and yet, I insist again,
These are not Men!

A Man is a man, who as a boy
Was at times both right and wrong
But who in growing became strong
And in his strength did find
A gentleness for all mankind.

A Man is a man, who through the years
Lives moments both short and long,
Learns that a heart can feel a song.
Grows to be great, yet kind,
Leaves smallness of youth behind.

He has a heart, this man
Big enough to understand.
He pulls himself together,
Lifts himself to stand
Because now, he is a Man!

By: Bert-Mary Brady

Painting by: Bert-Mary Brady

"My Man"

Copi

Where, oh where, is pretty little Copi?
Look at this terrible, terrible mess.
Where, oh where, is devilish Copi?
Down the hall in the bedroom I guess?

All curled up by the bed,
With a slipper under her head.
Dreaming dreams and scheming schemes,
That's where our little Copi girl is.

She likes to dream of Jim and Bert.
She likes to dream of ice cream for dessert.
She likes to dream of rolling in the grass,
That's our feisty little lass.

Come on Jim, let's go find her.
We'll just sneak right up behind her,
Tickle her ears and rub her tummy
Then we'll give her a yummy, yummy, yummy.

She is sometimes funny, sometimes coy,
Always bringing us lots of joy.
Our love, our buddy, our little pearl,
That's our special Copi girl!

By: Bert-Mary Brady

Copi

Painting by: Bert-Mary Brady

The Greeting

She sits so proud as she waits
For mom or dad at the gate,
Positioned so she can see
At first glance, which it will be.
Ready for that old welcome game,
The greeting always the same:
Three times around, jumping up and down
A pat on the head, then off to bed.

By: Bert-Mary Brady

Final Exit

How long has it been?
A year or a day?
I long for you so
Since you hastened away.

I used to be calm
And sensible, too,
Yet now I do nothing
But wait for you.

When I think of the way
The years must go by
Without touching your face
Or hearing your sigh.

I think that perhaps
I should take in my own hands,
The life that I'm left
To God's own plans.

But that would be foolish,
As well as unwise.
So I pray for patience
Of considerable size.

The only real comfort
That I have is to know,
That the passing of time
For you is not slow.

No longer in pain
But only in bliss
You wait for me now,
Since death places its kiss!

                        By: Bert-Mary Brady

Destiny

Broken and aching
My heart sheds tears.
You've gone away
And I'm left with fears.
Days are too long
And nights are oh, so cold.
I'm left here alone
With just our bands of gold.
Memories and dreams fill my head
At night as I go to bed,
Surrounding and warming me as
I turn my face into the pillow and softly sigh …
Good night, my love, I miss you so,
Or should I say,
Goodbye, for now, Goodbye!

By: Bert-Mary Brady

'Tis Midnight

One small light softly glowing
In a midst of music flowing
Nothing more to do today
Now sleep, sleep the night away.

Tomorrow brings sun or rain,
Happiness, sorrow, perhaps pain.
Cry not for yesterday,
Just sleep, sleep the night away.

Lost is a love you held so long.
Hurt swells with yesterday's song.
Dream not, I say
Best sleep, sleep the night away.

By: Bert-Mary Brady

Indulgence

I'm going to kick off my shoes
And wiggle my toes,
Put on my robe,
Won't hang up my clothes.
Snap off the lights
And lock every door,
Turn on some blues,
Stretch out on the floor.

Then I'll reach out for a match,
Light my cigarette
And just this once
Won't try to forget.
Maybe I'll cry,
Maybe I won't
No one will know
Whether I do or don't!

By: Bert-Mary Brady

Time

I have taught my lips to smile again,
I have taught my voice to laugh.
I have taught my eyes to cry again,
But my heart, who teaches that?

I have taught my ears to hear again,
I have taught my feet to dance.
I have taught my hands to work again,
But my heart, who teaches that?

I have taught my mind to think again,
I have taught my soul to pray.
I have taught myself to live again,
But my heart, who teaches that?

By: Bert-Mary Brady

Retrospect

The dishes wait somewhere,
Who cares? Not tonight.
The papers lay somewhere,
Who Cares? Not tonight.

Not tonight oh, not tonight,
Tomorrow, but not tonight.
Tomorrow I'll see somehow, and care.
Tomorrow I'll feel somehow, and care.

Not tonight, please not tonight,
Tomorrow, but not tonight.
Tonight I must go back, three years,
Each year, tonight I must go back!

By: Bert-Mary Brady

A New Outlook on Life

Many people, in various ways, have attempted to express life in words. Essays, poems and songs both classical and popular have been written in an attempt to define life. Yet, has anyone ever thought of life as being a dictionary? For, if you really think about it, there is a similarity.

Consider for a moment just what a dictionary really is. It is not merely a book, by all means. It is a piece of work with a beginning and end, created and formed with great care. It contains explanations and meanings for every work we could ever want to wonder about.

What is life? It too is a piece of work, having creation and form with beginning and end. Similarly for every question that one should ever need an answer to, an explanation can be found somewhere, sometime in past, present or future experiences in life.

When one leafs through a dictionary, each page places before him new words and concepts. As he goes on collecting these words and meanings, adding them to his vocabulary, he gains more power in the struggle or self-expression.

In the same light, as one passes through the pages of life, each day brings forth different experiences which, when used as a background, help to build the knowledge and understanding of a person. The more a person learns the more functional he becomes.

Therefore, one could say life is a dictionary. Not in that it is cut and dry or is in chronological order, but because it holds an answer or meaning to whatever one might question – as long as one is willing to look for it.

Just as what one obtains from a dictionary helps to build a tower of knowledge, so do the experiences of life help to construct this same tower. In doing so, it creates for themselves a monument in their intellectual worlds.

By: Bert-Mary Brady

Trixie

Glance behind those silky, pensive eyes,
With their sad, wistful look,
Listen to those whimpering sighs,
Waiting to capture your wounded heart,
Yet holding back a devilish spark,
Ready to pull you forward in life,
Because there's my foxy, little pixie,
Sweet, loving, cuddly Trixie!

By: Bert-Mary Brady

Ruth W. S. Coon

A Tribute

To my role model, my inspiration. The strongest person I have ever known. One who encouraged me, but never pushed. One who was always there to listen and showed such respect to everyone. The one who taught me how to face and cope with life's challenges and shared the skills I would need through life. She was so talented, so patient and always calm even in the midst of chaos. She was the best friend I ever had and still guides me as I move on, even though she is no longer here. My mother, my teacher, my Mom!

By: Bert-Mary Brady

Let me share of few of her creative thoughts:

What is Happiness?

How could you explain what Happiness was when your heart thumped at a smile from a man who smiled too rarely?
That it was hearing him speak, sharing his dreams, feeling his arms around you?
When these things were gone, then death had come.
Even though you ate and drank and answered questions,
you were dead too.
If you had such ecstasy and now it is gone.
To the one who means just this to me.

By: Ruth W.S. Coon 1939

The Caller

My daily caller,
A much too friendly wasp,
Flirts, caresses and then is off!
Searching new victims,
New souls to distress,
Someday he'll call
To meet with … Death!

By: Ruth W.S. Coon 1939

Were You There?

Drums, bugles, sifting through children's voices.
Years have passed since I have seen a small town parade.
I know no-one in this particular town.
I stop, not because of traffic but because of streams of
small town folk hurrying along.
Mothers calling out words of caution
Children laughing, pushing on ahead.
"Hi there, Betty, what time did you get here?"
"Did you see Grace? We'll meet you later."
Snatches of conversations make me feel alone
In the midst of all this warmth and friendliness.
I chat with a little freckled face boy ...
Sure, he has red hair cropped short.
Don't all small-freckled face boys have red hair?
I comfort a tiny girl, dressed in pink ruffles
Who for the moment seems lost.
Now I'm not alone.
Here's the parade!
Gay colors, flags, uniforms so clean and pressed.
Music, a brave attempt at least
Young and old ... a tempo of the light and the heavy.
The floats pass by one by one
Colorful and impressive.
Cars filled with senior citizens creep on
The music fades, the crowd begins to rustle
Then with great momentum seems to disappear
All in one direction.
My interest captured, had to follow ...
Follow baby carriages, babies toddling,

Babies, God Bless them, being carried here and there.
Some sleeping on their daddy's shoulders
Others less fortunate with wide eyes wondering what it's all about
What the noise of the "barker" means;
Others in carriages being pushed around …
There can't be much air down there.
Here is a baby having his bottle, not very sanitary,
But it keeps him from crying.
Oh, yes. Over the din of the Ferris wheel you can hear his cry.
The toddler, those dear little legs, so short, so tired by now
Wanders from one concession to another;
At last, the toy autos.
Some thought this was fun, others scary,
The gentle old man saunters round and round
Stretching forth his hand and saying,
"Tickets please." "No hurry here."
A child has lost his ticket.
"That's alright sonny, you just have a nice ride."
On to the Ferris wheel, way up high
It stops to load
Two little boys climb aboard, sitting with their dad between,
Legs too short to touch the floor,
The bar in front too far away to grab,
The only thing to do is to hold tight to dad.
See them draw in their breaths as they leave the ground
Their eyes pop out as they come around
I can see them clutching, holding fast,
The end is near.

They climb out.
Adults are asking, "Wasn't it fun? Did you like it?"
"Of course you did! You were big boys not to cry."
There they stand, two little boys about two and three,
Not even a smile!
The parents seem pleased and once more they start.
This time, without me!

By: Ruth W.S. Coon

www.ingramcontent.com/pod-product-compliance
Lightning Source LLC
Chambersburg PA
CBHW032020040426
42448CB00006B/675